Susanne Schaadt

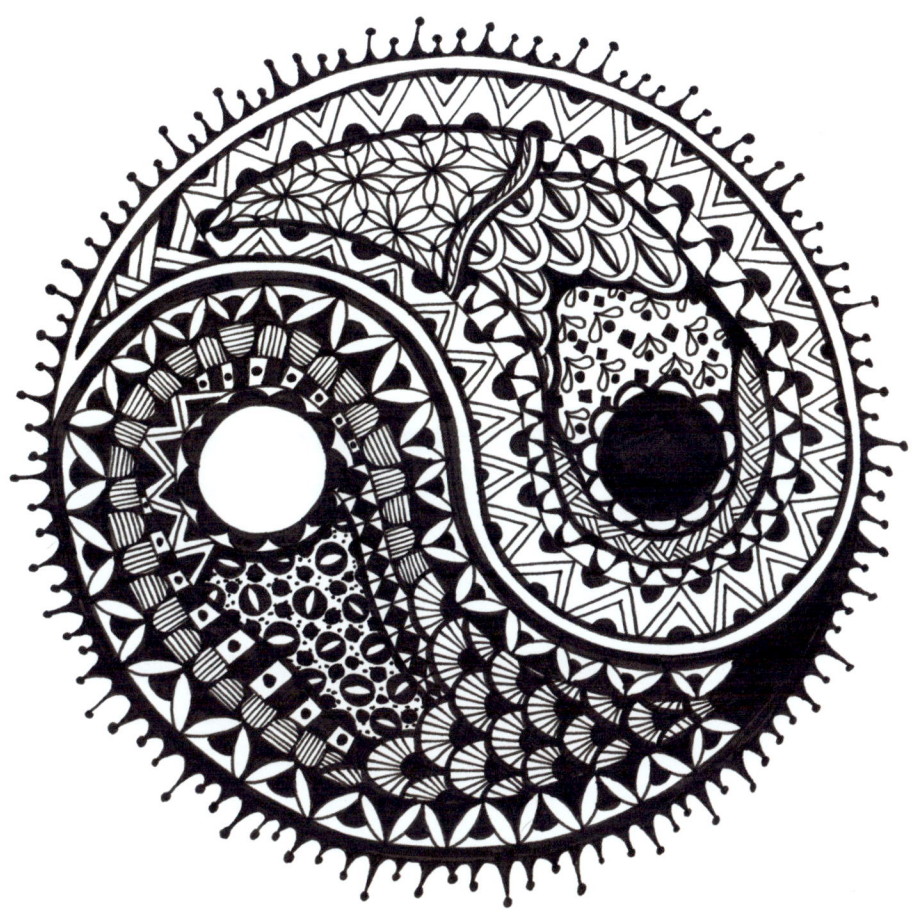

Meditative Zendoodles

A Treasure Trove of Relaxing Moments

4880 Lower Valley Road • Atglen, PA 19310

Other Schiffer Books on Related Subjects:

Painterly Days: The Flower Watercoloring Book for Adults, Kristy Rice, ISBN 978-0-7643-5091-7
Animal Life: Nature Mandala Coloring Book, Timothy Phelps, ISBN 978-0-7643-5278-2
Garden Life: Nature Mandala Coloring Book, Timothy Phelps, ISBN 978-0-7643-5279-9

Copyright © 2017 by Schiffer Publishing, Ltd.

Originally published as *Meditative Zendoodles* by Christophorus Verlag GmbH & Co. KG (c) 2015. Translated from the German by Omicron Language Solutions LLP.

Library of Congress Control Number: 2016961419

The methods in this book have been carefully created and tested by the author; however, they cannot undertake to guarantee them. Liability of the author or the publisher and their agents for personal, property, and pecuniary damage is excluded.

All rights reserved. No part of this work may be reproduced or used in any form or by any means—graphic, electronic, or mechanical, including photocopying or information storage and retrieval systems—without written permission from the publisher.

The scanning, uploading, and distribution of this book or any part thereof via the Internet or any other means without the permission of the publisher is illegal and punishable by law. Please purchase only authorized editions and do not participate in or encourage the electronic piracy of copyrighted materials.

"Schiffer," "Schiffer Publishing, Ltd.," and the pen and inkwell logo are registered trademarks of Schiffer Publishing, Ltd.

Photo credits: Portrait on jacket flap, pp. 10-11: © Susanne Schaadt;
p. 9: © FotoW / fotolia.com; pp. 68-69: © Frank Schuppelius
Product management and editing: Laura Lesum
Layout and lithography: Michael Feuerer

Type set in American Typewriter/Futura Std
ISBN: 978-0-7643-5289-8
Printed in China

Published by Schiffer Publishing, Ltd.
4880 Lower Valley Road
Atglen, PA 19310
Phone: (610) 593-1777; Fax: (610) 593-2002
E-mail: Info@schifferbooks.com
Web: www.schifferbooks.com

For our complete selection of fine books on this and related subjects, please visit our website at www.schifferbooks.com. You may also write for a free catalog.

Schiffer Publishing's titles are available at special discounts for bulk purchases for sales promotions or premiums. Special editions, including personalized covers, corporate imprints, and excerpts, can be created in large quantities for special needs. For more information, contact the publisher.

We are always looking for people to write books on new and related subjects. If you have an idea for a book, please contact us at proposals@schifferbooks.com.

Contents

Preface 7
Exercises for Relaxation 8
Materials 9
Searching for Inspiration 10
The Basic Pattern: Step by Step 12
   Surface Patterns 14
   Geometric Patterns 26
   Scatter Patterns 28
   Band Patterns 32

Zendoodles 38
   ABC Patterns 40
   Favorite Words and Sayings 42
   Symbols from Different Cultures 46
   From the World of Fashion 50
   Scenes 52
   Postcards 56
   Inchies 58
   Sweet Treats 60
   From the Animal Kingdom 62
   Backgrounds 66
   Zendoodling on Objects 68

Design Collection 70

Index of Patterns 78

Preface

Dear Reader,

What could be more wonderful than creative relaxation? Zendoodle—the meditative drawing method for young and old—offers you the opportunity (anytime, anywhere) to take a break from your everyday life and treat yourself to a little serenity and tranquility. Using pen and paper, simply let delicate patterns emerge. Stroke by stroke you create beautiful pieces of art. And it doesn't matter whether you can draw or not.

In our hectic, fast-paced world it isn't easy to find moments of peace and contemplation. Over-stimulation, demanding jobs, and everyday stress put a great burden on us. This makes regular breaks, when we can take a deep breath and regain our strength, all the more important.

Throughout my long career as a relaxation therapist, I have been teaching courses on Zendoodle drawing methods with great success. Children, adolescents, and adults are surprised and amazed by how easily they can draw decorative patterns, how much fun they have doing it, and how deeply they can relax with it. Since it is impossible to make mistakes with this creative therapy, everyone has their own personal sense of achievement. As a result, many of my participants have contracted "Zendoodle fever" and meditative Zendoodle drawing is now part of their daily ritual. If you like, you too can take a few minutes every day to turn off your stream of consciousness and, one line after another, immerse yourself in the world of Zendoodle patterns.

In just a few weeks you will have a notebook brimming with a wonderful collection of small creative works that are your drawings.

I wish you many relaxing and creative moments!

Yours,

S. Schaadt

Exercises for Relaxation

Drawing a Zendoodle pattern is a wonderfully simple and effective way to relax. It requires little preparation and practice, unlike other classic methods of relaxation. As an artist and relaxation therapist, I particularly appreciate the combination of creative work and relaxation. Again and again the meditative practice of drawing Zendoodle patterns presents an ideal way to do this.

Nevertheless, there may be times when you still might want to do something more to relax and relieve stress, or maybe you just don't have a pen and paper handy. For that I have provided you with some small and simple exercises that you can easily do—at home or at work—for some brief relaxation:

Shake It Out

Hold your arms out in front of you at shoulder width. Then, at a pace that is comfortable for you, begin to shake out your hands and arms. Shake all the stress away. If you like, bob your body up and down at the same time. Then shake out your legs. Sometimes, just 1–2 minutes of this exercise is sufficient for feeling fresher and more relaxed.

Hand Rubbing

Rub your palms together quickly until they feel really warm. Then place your palms on your face. Breathe in and out quietly and gently. Think about how your warm palms feel on your face. Where do you feel the most warmth? Repeat the exercise as many times as you like.

Pattern Immersion

Select a Zendoodle pattern that you particularly like. Contemplate the pattern very carefully. Where do the lines run? Follow the lines of the pattern with your eyes.

Now close your eyes and imagine the pattern covering the surfaces of the room. Perhaps it spreads out on the floor like a carpet or it runs over the walls like wallpaper. Let the expanding pattern comfort you and become as large as you can imagine it. When you are relaxed, open your eyes and stretch your muscles.

Materials

All you need for meditative drawing is a pen and a sheet of paper!

Good quality 80 or 110 lb (120 or 160 gsm) printer paper is my favorite. For pens, commercial fineliners (0.4 mm and 0.8 mm) work wonderfully for both black and white as well as colorful Zendoodles. The 0.4 mm pen easily produces delicate lines and strokes for even the finest patterns. Pens with 0.8 mm-wide tips are better suited for filling in larger areas. The larger tips are also good for heavily tracing over contour lines to delineate the different areas of the pattern. Finally, use colored fineliners to draw patterns directly into a template or add color to negative space in the pattern.

In addition to pen and paper, another recommended tool is a soft pencil (grade B) or crayons. These are great for shading and adding dimensionality to the edges of your pattern.

When it comes to adding color, another medium that works well is watercolor pencils and watercolors. However, if you want to color a drawing with watercolors after using fineliners, make sure the fineliners are waterproof—otherwise the drawing may run. In addition, smooth watercolor paper works best when incorporating watercolors.

Finally, it is easier to add a background color to your work before drawing the pattern. To create intense, brilliant backgrounds, one technique I use is to extract pigment from watercolor pencils with water and apply the color to the paper with a brush. After the paint has dried, you can continue to draw as usual with a black or color fine-liner.

Searching for Inspiration

If you make a conscious effort you will discover shapes, structures, and patterns in your surroundings throughout the day. With a little skill and creativity you can use these to develop new Zendoodle patterns. The following pages offer step by step ways to turn simple, everyday objects into patterns. Let your imagination run wild to help you find inspiration in your surroundings!

To get started, think about the countless items you encounter every day—many of these offer great ideas and forms to build from. For example, think about the wonderful patterns in a head of cabbage, a piece of celery, the inside of an orange, a piece of star anise, parquet floors, pavement, embroidery, and fabric. These can all serve as the basis for decorative new patterns.

There are no limits to imagination and creativity when creating elegant Zendoodle patterns. Simply sketch the lines and shapes of an object and repeat or expand them until you have an interesting pattern.

Tip
You can draw inspiration from everything—an abacus in your child's classroom, a brush from the bathroom, or the basket in the kitchen!

Basket

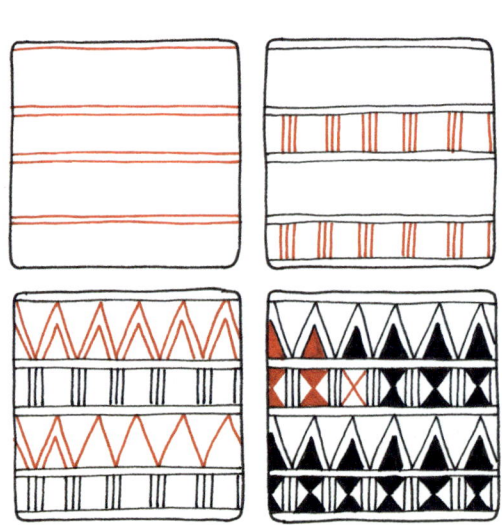

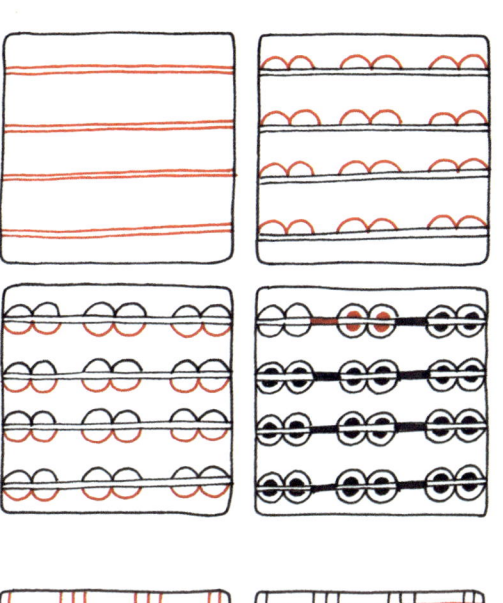
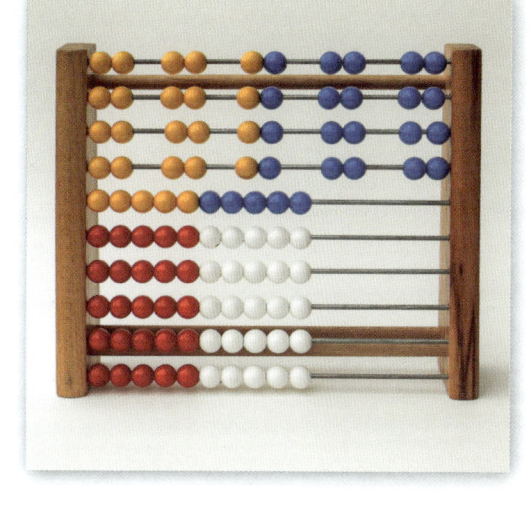

Abacus

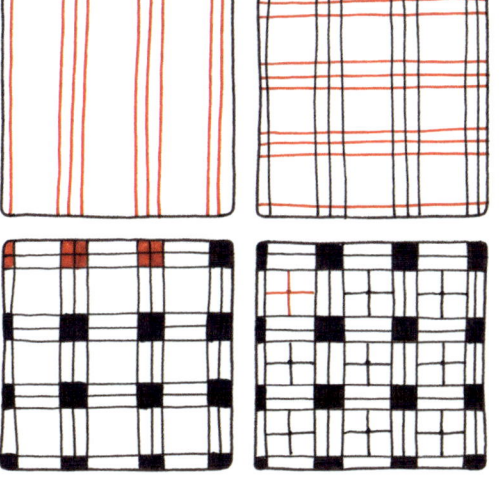

Embroidery

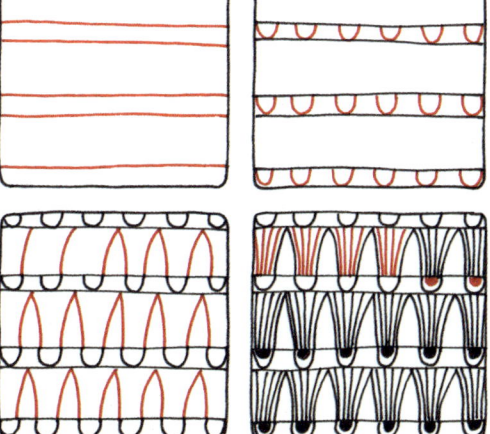
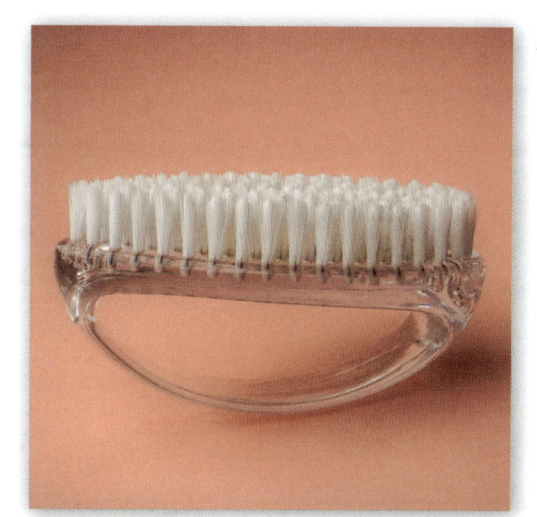

Brush

The Basic Pattern: Step by Step

Patterns, patterns, patterns—the possibilities are endless. In this chapter you will learn about different patterns by tracing samples step by step. Each pattern has four clear steps; the lines and surface areas to be added in each step are marked in red. Included here are examples of geometric patterns, as well as scatter patterns and bands.

Along with the step-by-step sequence for each of these popular patterns, I've also included a finished sample that shows the many things you can do with an individual pattern. You can add variation and color to your patterns, for example, by starting your pattern with a colored pen or by simply coloring in the negative spaces with your favorite colors. In some pictures I enhanced the pattern by applying a color background with watercolors or crayons before drawing. So, after being inspired by following the examples below, let loose and create patterns that reflect your personal aesthetic freely and spontaneously.

Surface Patterns

Surface patterns, just as the name suggests, are wonderfully suited for filling in an entire area or a large surface. In many cases, they are based on a simple, gridded pattern. All surface patterns are very flexible in that they can be extended indefinitely to add design to very large areas. Imagine an entire wall or a carpet covered in one pattern! But surface patterns aren't suitable just for rectangular areas, they also fit very well into round, oval, and free-form shapes. When thinking about ideas for your own surface patterns, look to nature or ornaments and decorations from different cultures, such as Persian rugs, stained glass windows, and Indian textiles.

Forest

Rescue

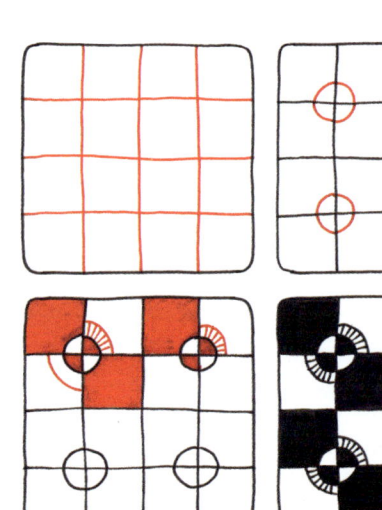

Belt

Swimming Pool

Peacock

Garden Party

Honey

Slices

Square

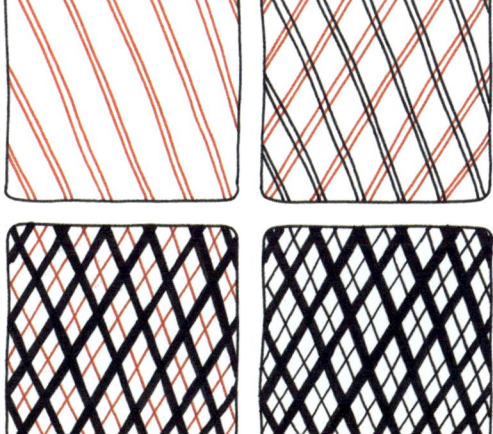

Glass

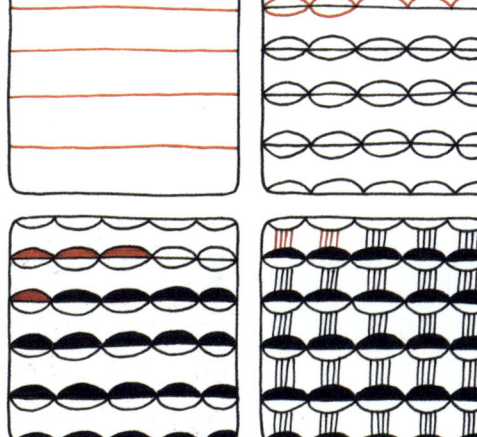
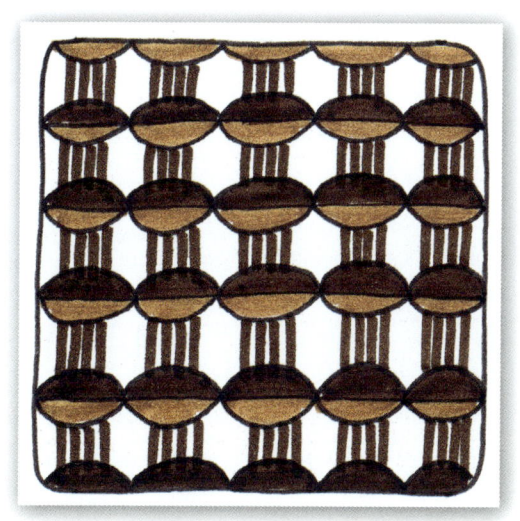
Tree House

Beach

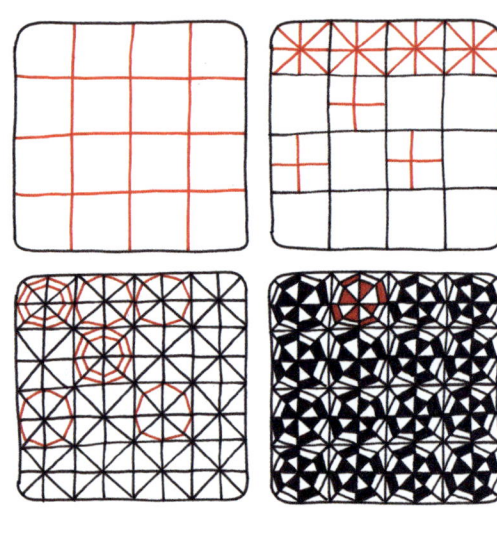

Mountain Peak

Fun

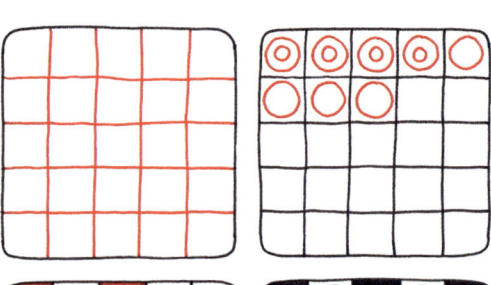
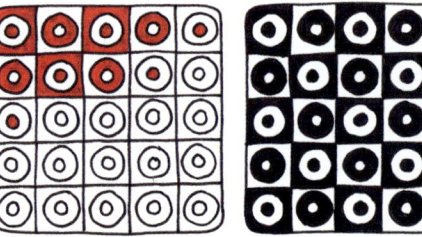

18

Cassette

Cheerfulness

Serrations

Wood

Blossoming

Chair Back

Leap

Fern

Reflection

Anemone

Musical Glass

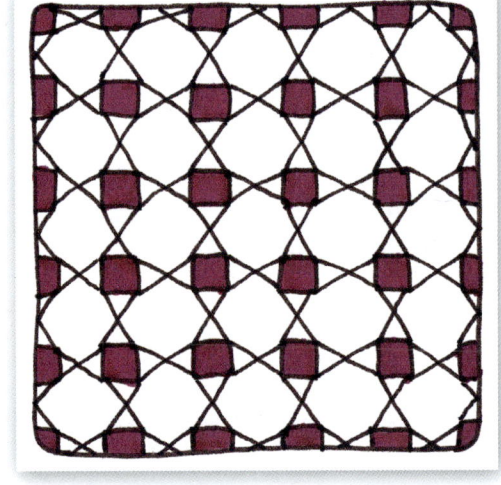

Desert

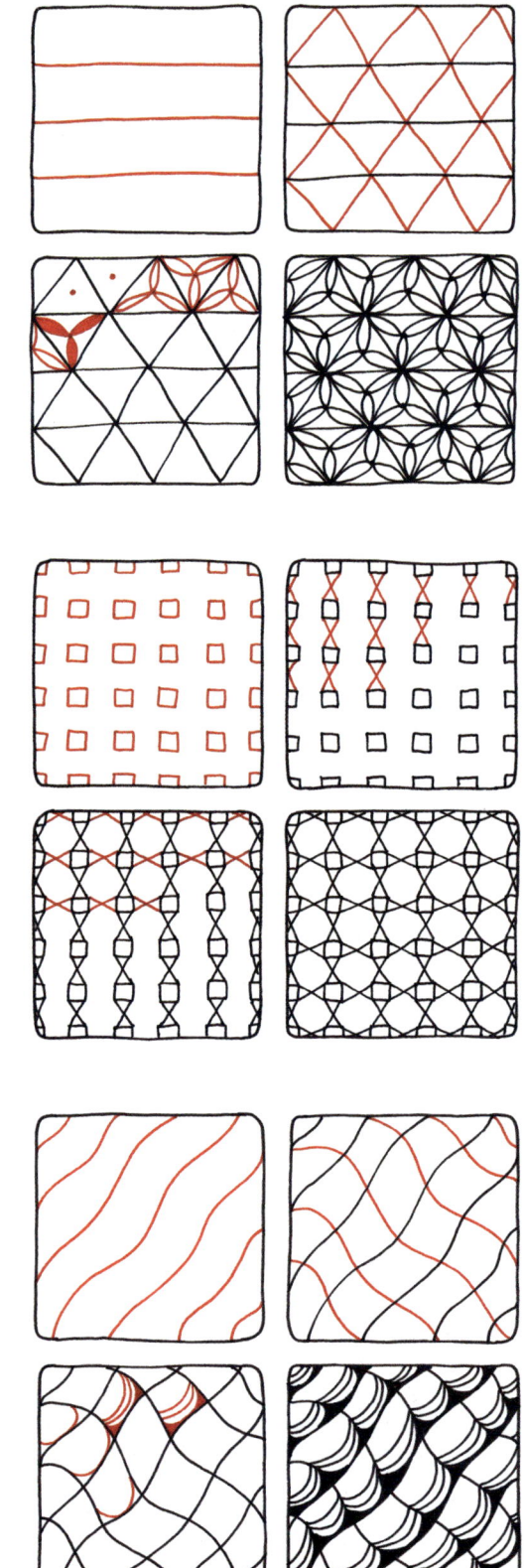

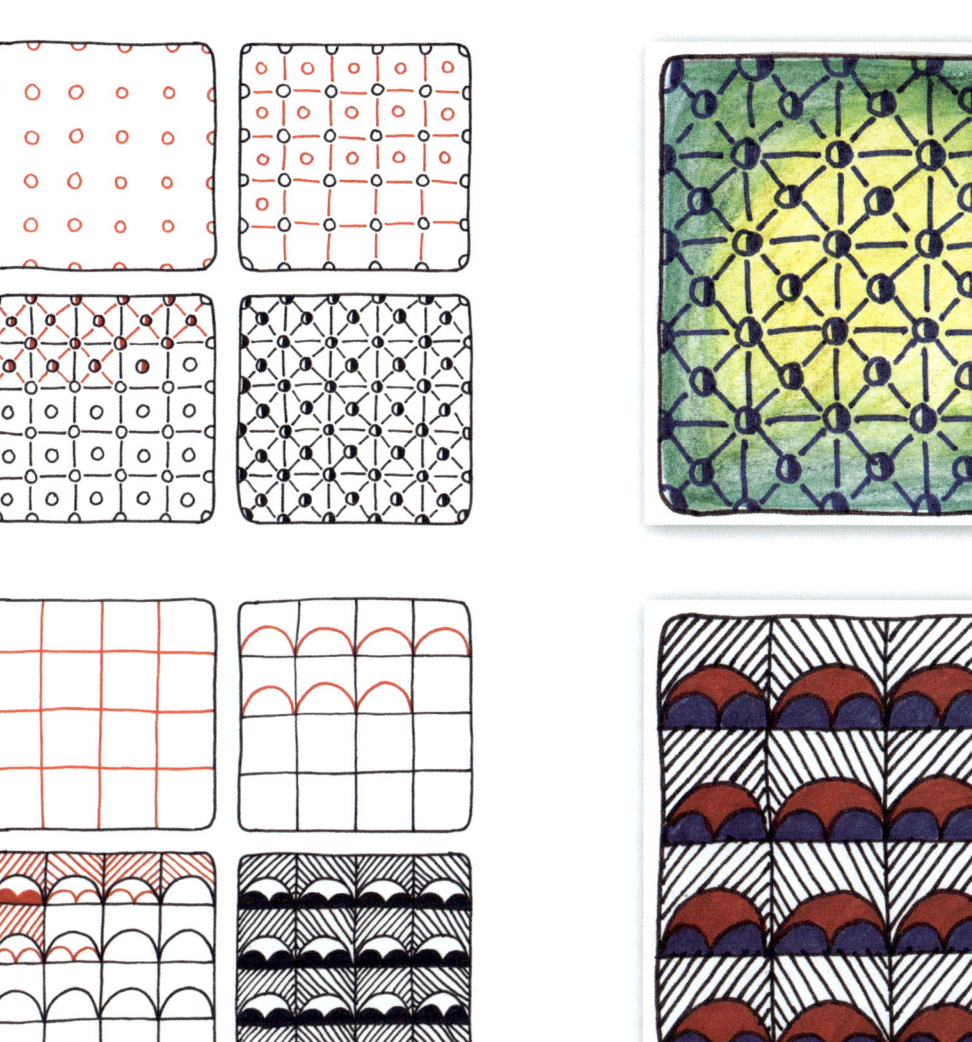

Game

Movie Theater

Salamander

Pencil

Park

Carpet

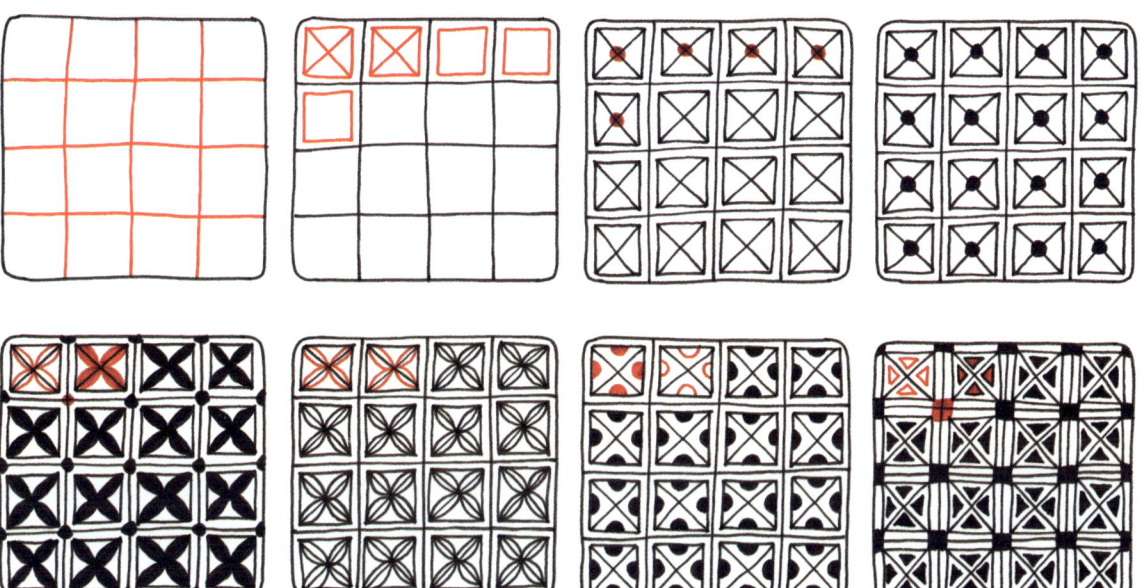

Fence

Kitchen

Geometric Patterns

Geometric patterns are very popular in my courses—even though they look somewhat complicated. Nevertheless, they are fantastically effective and easy to draw, contrary to expectations! With just a little bit of practice you can easily conjure these geometric marvels, stroke by stroke. It is best to start in the bottom left corner and follow the path of each red arrow in the diagrams below one line after another. Always end each stroke close to the corner you are drawing towards.

To create a variation on these patterns, instead of starting in the bottom left corner, try starting your pattern in a different corner. This will create a completely different effect, especially if you alternate the starting point when creating a composition with a number of triangles or squares next to each other in a band. You can also stack these patterns in a grid to create a surface pattern (see right).

Another way to vary geometric patterns is to create a pattern with right triangles in a rectangle instead of equilateral triangles. This will produce a somewhat compressed pattern. You can achieve a similar result by using rectangles instead of squares as your basic shape.

Triangle

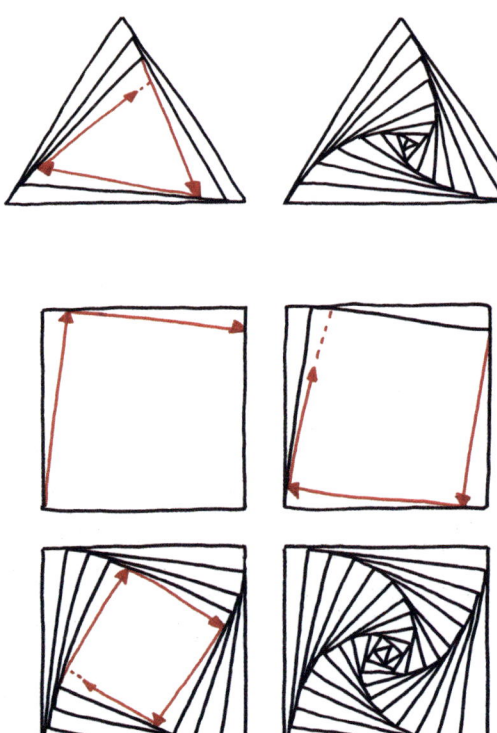

Square

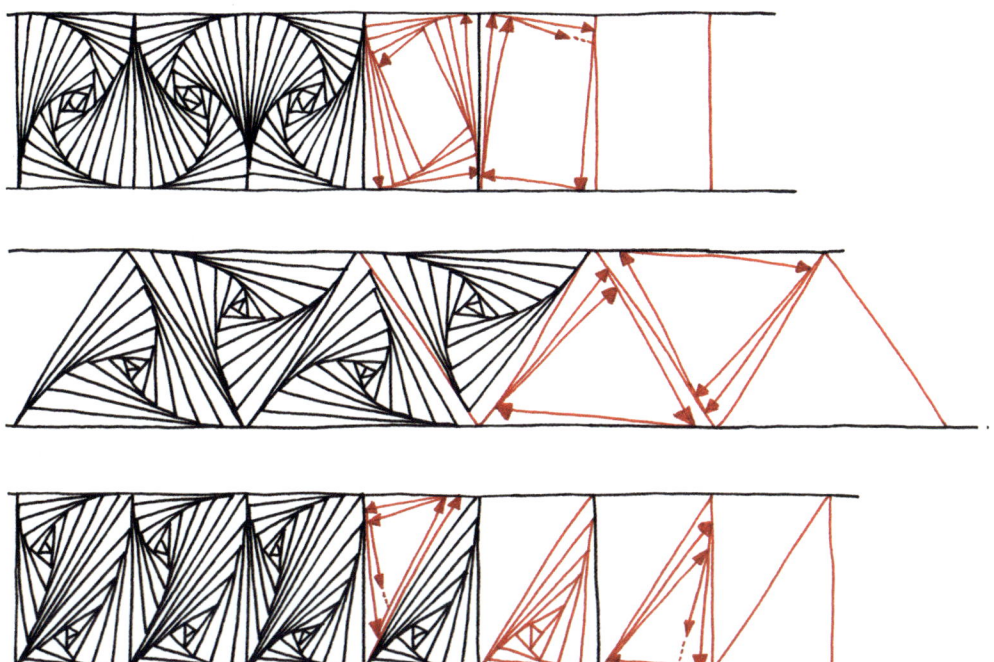

Create a band with side-by-side geometric patterns. Just use a rectangle instead of a square or a right triangle instead of an equilateral triangle. Alternating the starting point of your pattern also creates a different effect.

Tip
Geometric patterns offer very creative ways to add color. Plus it is a lot of fun. Give it a try!

Scatter Patterns

Many small individual shapes, spread loosely over a surface, create a scatter pattern. Whether you distribute the parts of the pattern evenly or concentrate them to one point in the surface area, they always seem light and playful. Scatter patterns lend themselves well to both small, irregular surfaces, as well as large areas. Coloring in the individual shapes or the background gives the scatter patterns a special charm.

Since many scatter patterns are made up of simple shapes, an illustration alone can explain them fully. The more complicated patterns are explained in several steps.

> **Tip**
> What is your favorite flower, character, or animal? All of these are great starting points for creating scatter patterns!

Universe

 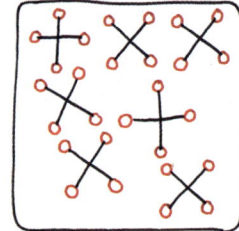
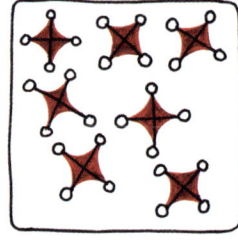 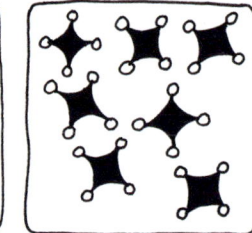

Juggler

Hush

 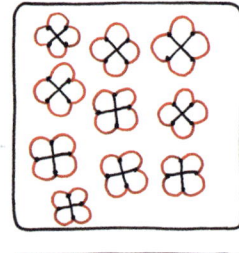
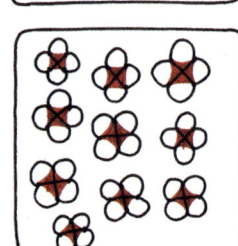 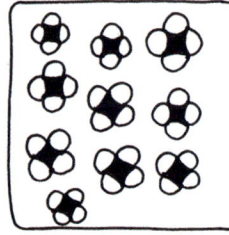

Little Flower

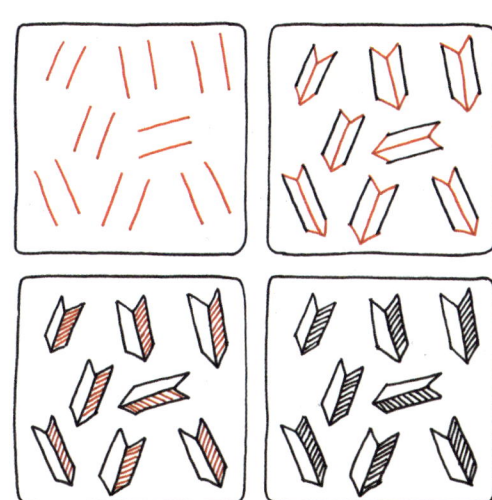

Playing Card

Paper Airplane

Gerber Daisy

Heart

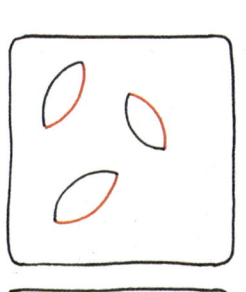

Light Bulb

Football

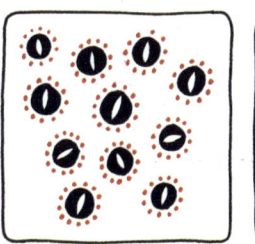
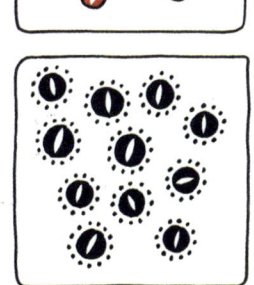

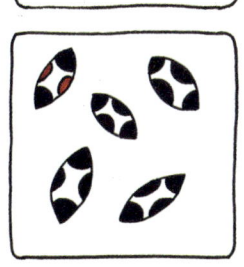

29

Gemstone

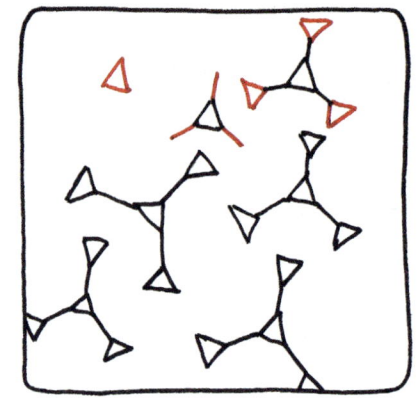
Electricity

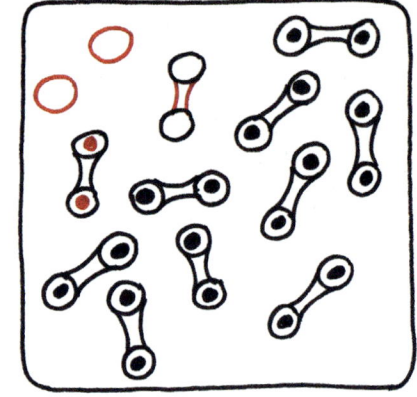
Dumbbell

Tunnel

Canoe

Mustache

Campground

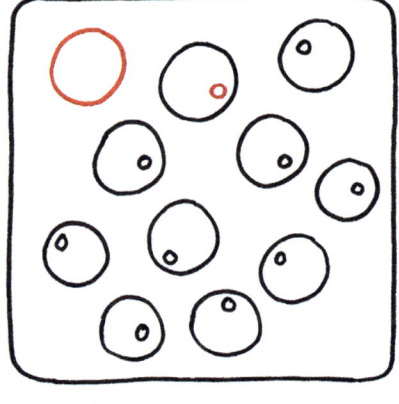
Tomato

Dance

Croissant

Angel

Ornament

Fantasy

Clasp

Fire

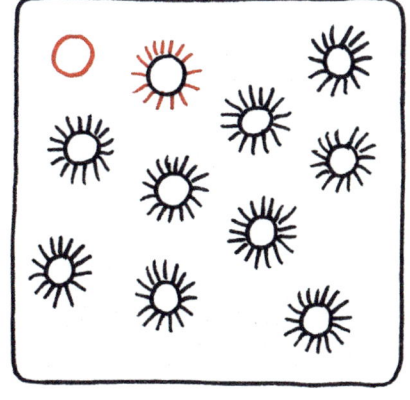
Rays

Herb

Moon

31

Band Patterns

Band patterns are among my favorite patterns. They are quite versatile. You can use them as simple decorative strips or you can create a surface pattern by combining several bands above and below or next to each other. The following drawings easily explain these patterns and how to work with them. Follow the red lines and surface areas from left to right to see each new step. The right section of each band shows a completed pattern.

The parallel lines that define the top and bottom of the band pattern can be straight or curved. Also, these lines can converge, so that the gap between them becomes narrower. When drawing a band pattern, always create your top and bottom lines first before you draw the pattern itself.

 Rails

 Waves

 Rickrack

 Sand

 Decor

 Darts

Scissors

Honeycomb

Letter

Sheet Music

Steps

Pressure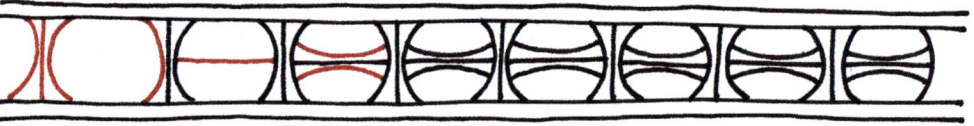

 Indian

 Wind

 Tower

 Spring

 Laurel

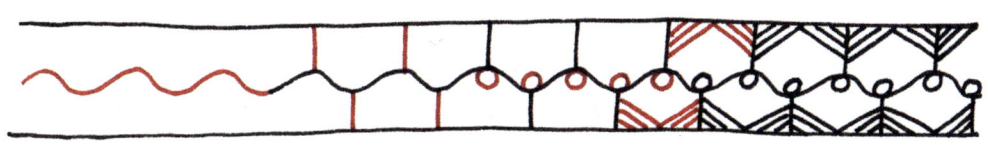 Curtain

Strips

Bird

Multitude

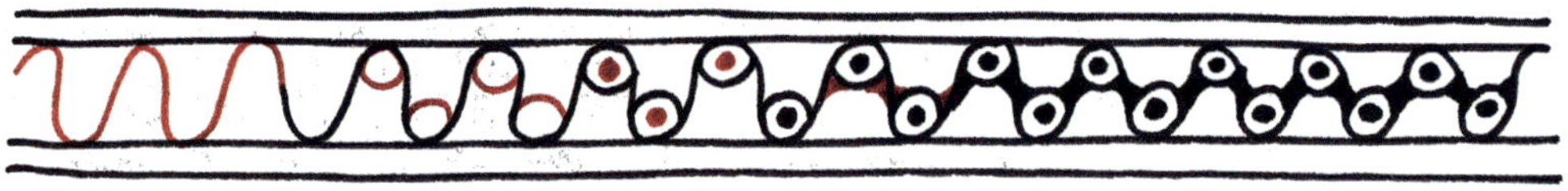

Braid

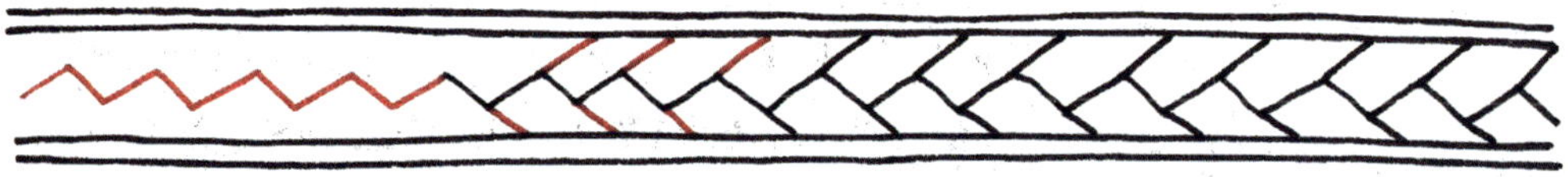

Start

Thunderstorm

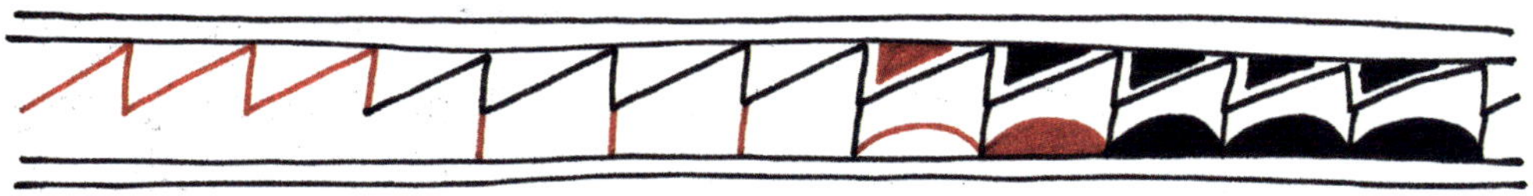

 Roof

 Rotation

 Beams

 Ringlet

 Cherry

 Sailor's Yarn

Zendoodles

Drawing Zendoodles is widely popular, perhaps because it offers endless possibilities and countless design ideas for adults and children. In the following pages you will find my favorite designs—I hope they give you a lot of enjoyment. Simply use the templates to easily trace the images, pattern for pattern, or fill them in with your own pattern creations.

For quick designs that don't require much time, consider the smaller patterns. Of course the larger ones can take a few hours to complete. But taking your time with these drawings is a very important component to the meditative nature of these creations. Also, you don't need to complete these motifs in one day, give yourself time. When drawing Zendoodles, enjoying the creative process and relaxing come first—the journey is its own reward.

I find it especially fun to conceptualize and draw the sayings and words, as well as design postcards. The postcards offer great opportunities to try new designs and colors and make great personal gifts and greeting cards. Perhaps you have a particular saying or quote that you would like to decorate with imaginative patterns!

ABC Patterns

Whether you design the letters, the background, or both with patterns, Zendoodle letters are very charming. Black and white or in color, they are very decorative and can adorn letterhead, journals, day planners, or a special note. And what could be more personal than a child's birthday card adorned with the child's Zendoodled first initial? You will find templates for ABC patterns on page 72.

Band patterns are ideal for filling in letters. For example, the "Labyrinth" pattern (page 32) looks great in the letter "J." Surface patterns, such as the "Chair Back" pattern (page 20) for "T," are also good choices.

Favorite Words and Sayings

I love sayings and beautiful words. They can express a feeling or life motto and quickly become eye-catchers when you add fantastic Zendoodle patterns. You can make great decorations to enhance your home as individual wall decorations or as a framed picture. Use the same techniques to inscribe Zendoodled words and sayings on a simple wooden board to make signs to hang on doors, walls, or decorate your work space. You will find templates for these designs on pages 72–73.

Colored fineliners are the best tool to use for these words and sayings. Draw and fill in the pattern in one color or add multiple colors throughout your design.

KEEP SMILING

HAPPY BIRTHDAY

DREAM

Aphorisms and maxims are ubiquitous in home decor. Lovingly designed, they encourage us and allow us to create strength and energy. So, at the end of a hectic day, simply design your favorite quote or a great saying!

Surface patterns such as "Leap" and "Anemone" (pages 21-22), make good ornamental frames.

Symbols from Different Cultures

Almost every culture has its own set of wonderfully embellished symbols, emblems, and sacred signs. In the Celtic tradition, besides pieces of jewelry and vessels decorated with fine patterns and ornamentation, we also find artfully worked crosses. Throughout many centuries these crosses have retained their mystical and mysterious aesthetics.

This cross features four geometric triangles added to the centerpiece of a Celtic cross (page 26).

In many Arab countries, the Hand of Fatima is considered a symbol of protection against the evil eye. In the Western world, it has become a popular fashion accessory. The eye in the palm is characteristic of this form. Here the "Spring" band pattern (page 35) fills in the eyelids.

The peace sign is timeless and always relevant. Ever since it was developed in 1958 as a symbol advocating for nuclear disarmament, this has been the world's best-known symbol for peace. In addition to surface patterns ("Peacock," page 15), I used band patterns ("Sheet Music," page 34) for this peace sign.

48

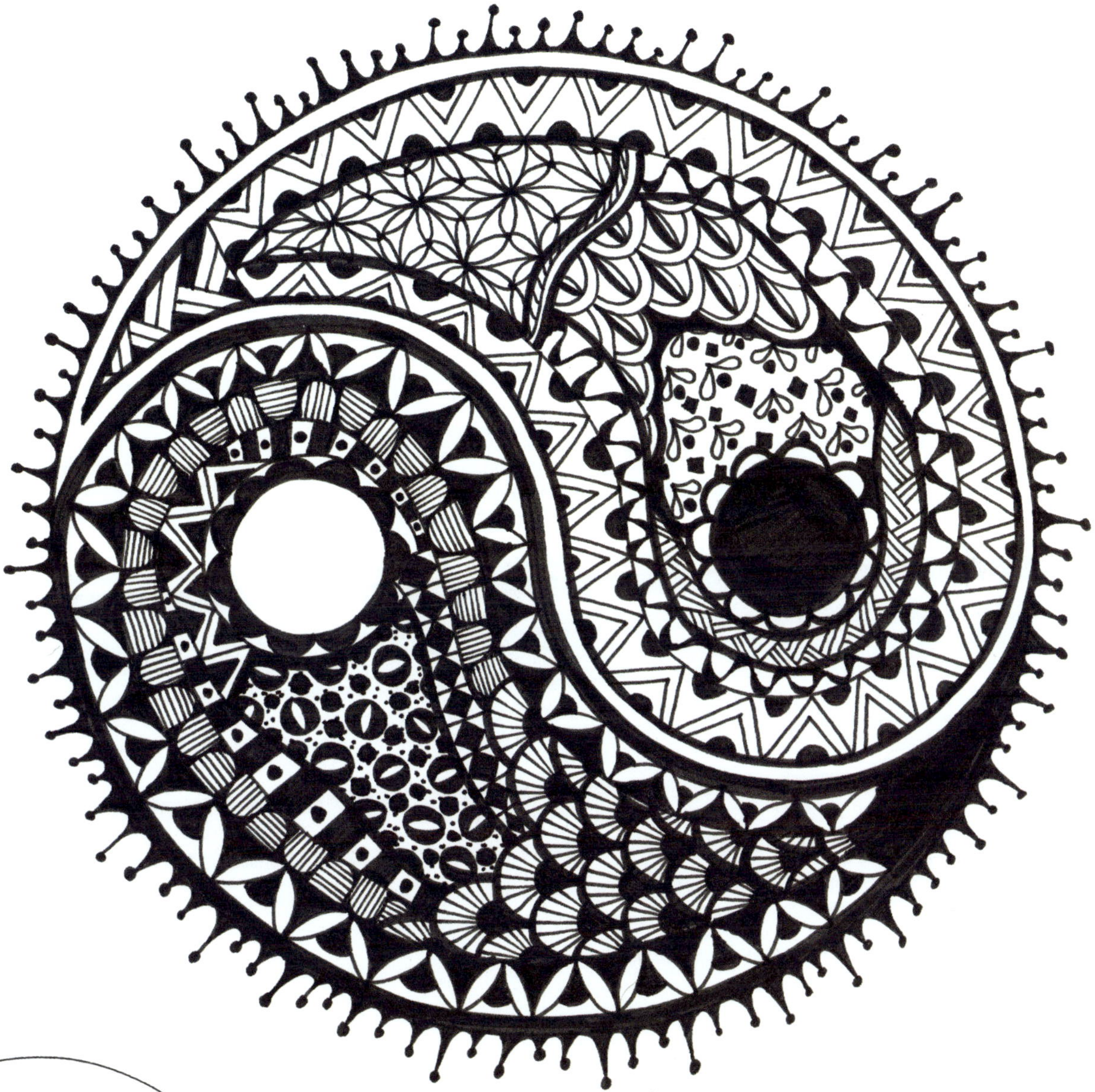

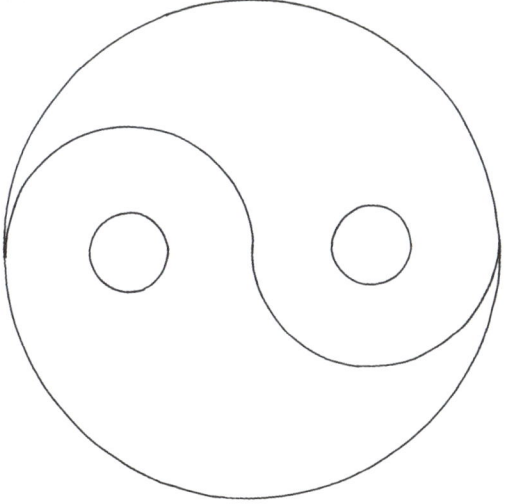

Yin and Yang are derived from Chinese culture and symbolize two complementary elements, inseparable from each other, and balanced with each other—the prerequisite for all life. To illustrate the dark half, use a highly detailed pattern or fill in the gaps with black.

49

From the World of Fashion

The world of fashion is alive with colors, shapes, and especially patterns! It is difficult to imagine something fashionable without decorative patterns and ornaments, whether through embroidery, lace, textile designs, or accessories. With this in mind, here you will find templates and examples of garments and fashion accessories for Zendoodle drawing!

It could be that you can add Zendoodle patterns to just about everything. Even this simple umbrella is poised for your decorative creativity.

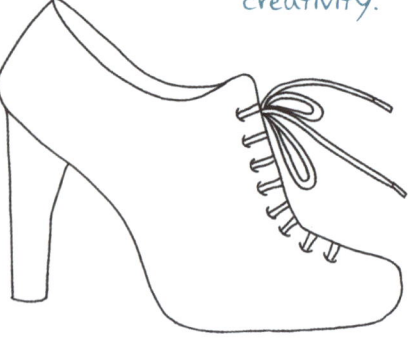

This shoe is a beautiful combination of surface and band patterns. The "Serrations" pattern (page 19) offers a particularly interesting effect in the middle of the shoe!

Here, the patterns make this dress even more fun and festive. Simply fill in each layer with a different pattern: "Peacock," "Blossoming," "Leap," or "Fern" (pages 15, 20-21).

Scenes

Once you are comfortable creating patterns, expand your canvas by incorporating Zendoodles into small works of art or even whole pictures created with patterns. Here are some suggestions of what you can accomplish with multiple patterns, but don't limit your imagination!

Relax as you draw an underwater landscape, a flowery meadow, a joyful sun, or a sparkling starry sky.

You can draw many different Zendoodle patterns into this sun's rays. Finish with playful spirals at the end of the rays to make the sun even more cheerful.

The hilly landscape between the trees shows how many ways Zendoodle patterns can be used. Surface and band patterns nestle among the twigs and branches and form the leafy crowns of trees. I used a brown fine-liner for the tree trunks.

The delicate, blue and green wings of these dragonflies give us a magical glimpse at summer. These colorfully decorated insects contrast nicely with the black and white crescent.

Zendoodle fish in this underwater world create a refreshing motif for meditative drawings. The water was created with the scatter pattern "Rays" (page 31).

Postcards

People love receiving personal greetings, especially when they arrive in the form of a custom postcard with an artfully designed message. This is the perfect way to tell someone you are thinking of them. Templates for postcards are shown on page 70. If you are drawing on paper, simply glue your Zendoodle to a piece of cardboard for backing.

Tip
Decorate the edges of your postcard with an exciting band pattern.

"Musical Glass" (page 22) is a particularly beautiful pattern, so I've used it here for the entire background.

56

If you don't want to write the letters yourself, simply print them from your computer. Then cut them out and stick them on your card.

Inchies

Little, but nice! Inchies are especially good for taking a break, whether during your lunch break, sitting in a waiting room, or even between larger Zendoodle projects. Because of their diminutive size they are quick and easy to fill with great patterns. They also bring joy and relaxation to everyone who draws. Mix it up by adding a little color here and there!

59

Sweet Treats

Mmmm...delicious! Who doesn't love a little treat now and then? Just by drawing sweet treats your mouth may start to water. Not only that, coloring your patterns with bright, cheerful colors will put you in a good mood. These designs are ideal for creating invitations or place setting cards with pizzazz!

Decorate this sweet cupcake with the band patterns "Decor," "Darts," and "Laurel" (pages 33 & 35) and the surface pattern "Honey" (page 16).

Tip
Fruit, dishes, and herbs also make terrific design templates. Frame your finished pieces to make great decorations for your kitchen.

For candy, you can use any basic shape and fill them in to suit your mood. The round candy features "Gerber Daisy" (page 29) and the square one the "Kitchen" pattern (page 25).

From the Animal Kingdom

Animals are extremely popular subjects for drawings of all sizes, so we won't forget them here! Your colored pencils and pens should get a workout with these motifs—what would a toucan or a delicate hummingbird be without their dazzling colors?

> **Tip**
> Animals make great wall tattoos. Decorate your room with critters of all stripes.

The different shades of green in this intricate pattern create a helpful camouflage for this lizard, keeping it safe amongst the green leaves of the jungle. Pay attention to the creature's long, sweeping tail.

This gorgeous, dazzling toucan lives in the treetops of the tropical rainforest and stands out in wonderful contrast to its surroundings. To finish the piece I add color to the negative space created by the black lines of the pattern.

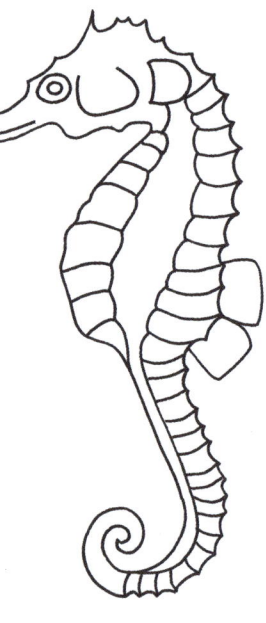

The delicate shape of a sea horse lends itself particularly well to band patterns, including "Letter" and "Strips" (pages 34 & 36). As I did with the lizard, I drew the patterns for this sea horse with colored fineliners. These bright colors give the design a light and airy feeling.

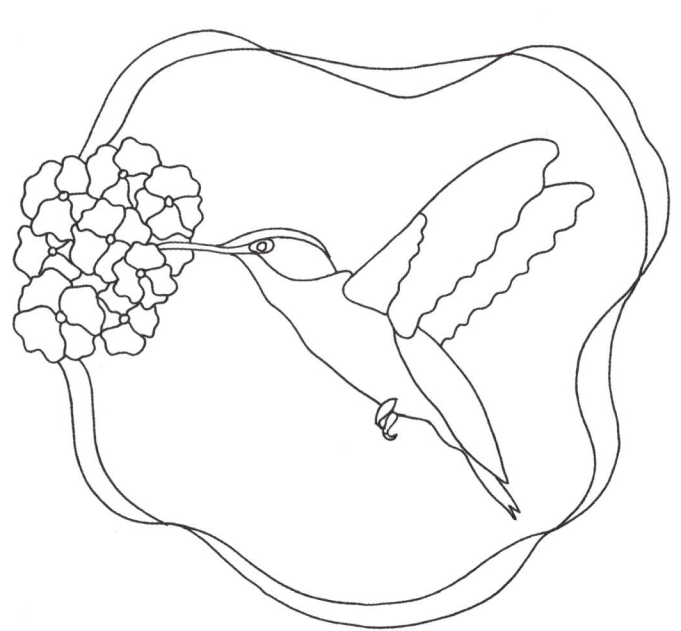

Tip
To create a larger canvas for your drawings, use a copy machine to enlarge the size of the templates when reproducing them.

A hummingbird drinking nectar from a flower is one of my favorite designs. The green band sways gently, as if moving in a gentle breeze, and gives the hummingbird a protective frame. The delicate pink, yellow, and orange flowers create a lovely contrast to the hummingbird, drawn in blue, green, and turquoise tones.

Backgrounds

Experiment with different backgrounds for your patterns. Old maps, pages from old books or newspapers, and pages of poetry are excellent backgrounds for Zendoodles. It is a lot of fun to draw on these non-traditional papers and match your designs and patterns to the themes in the background. This approach creates extraordinary images. Place your piece in a matching frame to create a great accent piece for any room.

An old nautical chart serves as the background for this Zendoodle. To match the maritime theme, I drew a sail boat as a Zendoodle. For the sails I used surface patterns, including "Peacock" and "Serrations" (pages 15 & 19).

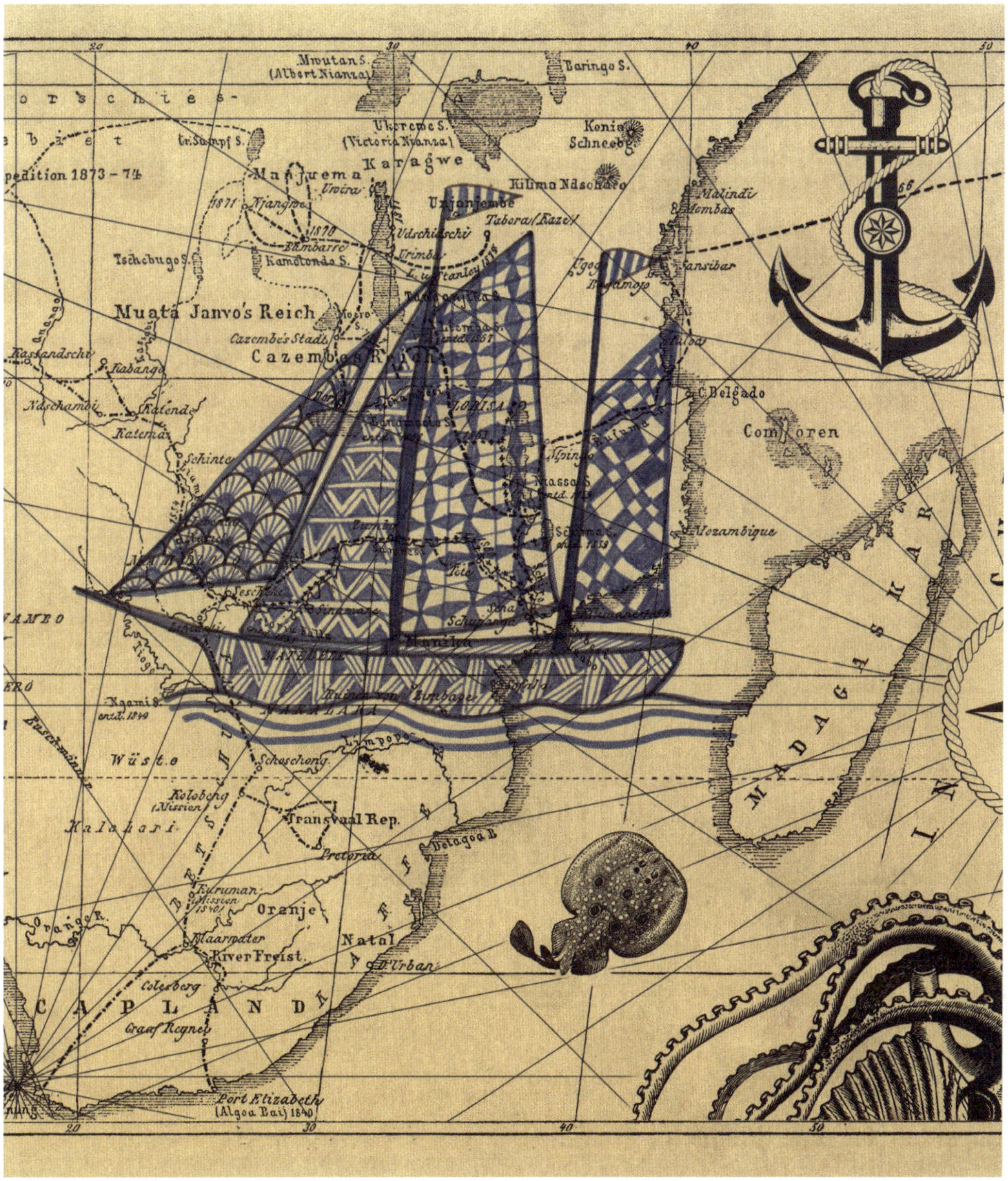

Zendoodling on Objects

The most important thing about drawing Zendoodles, is the simple act of drawing—the joy of creating and experiencing relaxing moments. But over the years many of my students have asked me what they should do with all the Zendoodles they have created. My advice is always: keep them! You can keep your drawings in a folder or fasten them in a binder. However, for some of them, it would be quite a shame if they simply disappeared from sight. They are much too beautiful for that!

There are many other ways that you can use these small works of art. Many of my Zendoodles adorn such things as letterhead, bookmarks, CD cases, and greeting cards. To do this, I simply trim the drawings to fit and glue them on.

Create your own personal Zen garden with Zendoodle stones and fine sand!

A practical and especially pleasing way to keep your Zendoodles in view every day is to make a Zendoodle calendar (see below). Simply tape or glue your favorite designs onto a blank, create-your-own calendar. This way, you can enjoy your Zendoodles every week or every month.

With just a little bit of drawing experience you can even create patterns directly on objects. Make sure to use a waterproof fine-liner when decorating diaries, photo frames, or other items.

Tip
When you draw on stone or wood, pay attention to the surface. It is best to test the pen's line thickness and contours on a less visible place before you start on your final creation.

Design Collection

On the following pages, you will find templates for the designs on pages 6, 40–45, 56–57, and 60–61. I'm including additional templates that I've created over time. These will get you started with a variety of basic forms for your Zendoodles. To scale the templates up, simply enlarge the templates to the desired size on a copier. Make sure to use 80 or 110 lb (120 or 160 gsm) copy paper for your creations.

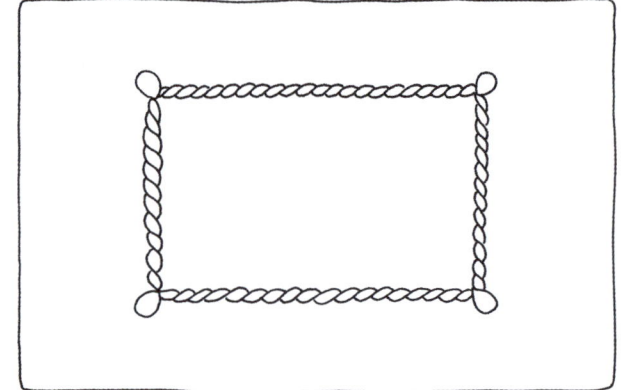

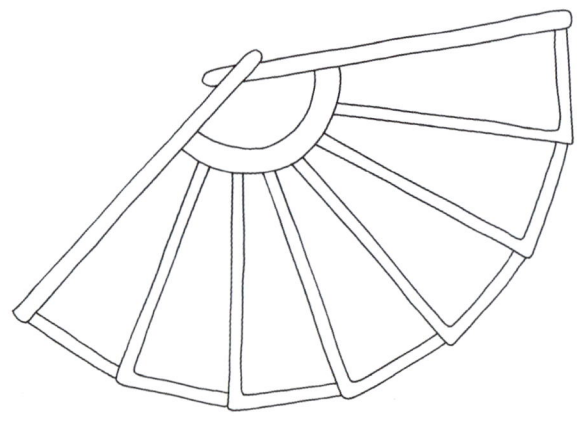

A	B	C	D
E	F	G	H
I	J	K	L
M	N	O	P
Q	R	S	T
U	V	W	X
Y	Z		

LOVE

PEACE

LUCK

PAUSE

KEEP SMILING

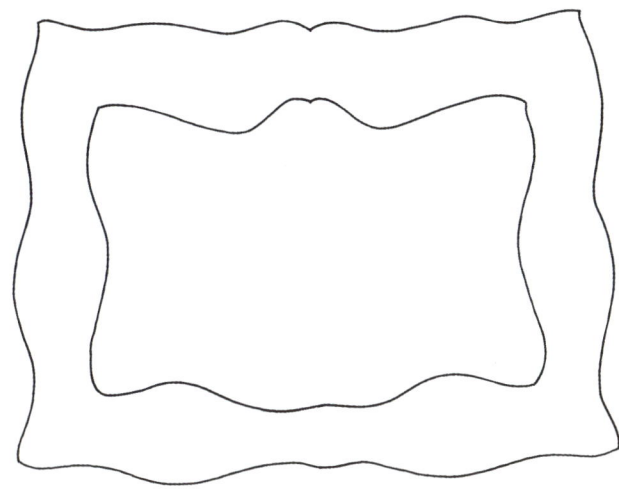

HAPPY BIRTHDAY

DREAM

FRIEND
FREE
TRUTH

keep calm & feel good

73

BE HAPPY HAVE FUN

Index of Patterns

Here you will find all the patterns again in a thumbnail reference. Use this index to quickly select the patterns you are interested in using, then find the detailed step-by-step guide for each respective pattern on the page referenced.

Basket page 10	Abacus page 11	Embroidery page 11	Brush page 11	Forest page 14	Rescue page 14	Belt page 15	Swimming Pool page 15
Peacock page 15	Garden Party page 16	Honey page 16	Slices page 16	Square page 17	Glass page 17	Tree House page 17	Beach page 18
Mountain Peak page 18	Fun page 18	Cassette page 19	Cheerfulness page 19	Serrations page 19	Wood page 20	Blossoming page 20	Chair Back page 20
Leap page 21	Fern page 21	Reflection page 21	Anemone page 22	Musical Glass page 22	Desert page 22	Game page 23	Movie Theater page 23
Salamander page 23	Pencil page 24	Park page 24	Carpet page 24	Fence page 25	Kitchen page 25	Triangle page 26	Square page 26
Universe page 28	Juggler page 28	Husk page 28	Little Flower page 28	Playing Card page 29	Paper Airplane page 29	Gerber Daisy page 29	Heart page 29

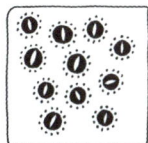 Light Bulb page 29	 Football page 29	 Gemstone page 30	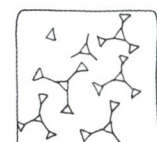 Electricity page 30	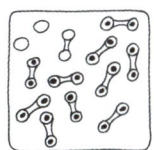 Dumbbell page 30	 Tunnel page 30	 Canoe page 30	 Mustache page 30
 Campground page 30	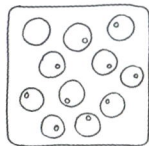 Tomato page 30	 Dance page 30	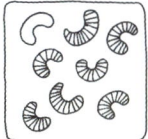 Croissant page 31	 Angel page 31	 Ornament page 31	 Fantasy page 31	 Clasp page 31
 Fire page 31	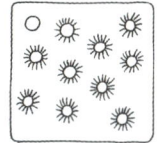 Rays page 31	 Herb page 31	 Moon page 31	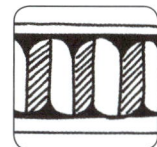 Train page 32	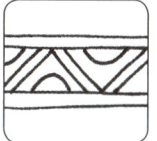 Clown page 32	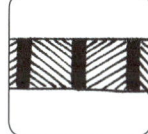 Rainforest page 32	 Labyrinth page 32
 Rails page 33	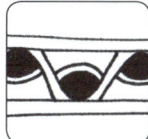 Waves page 33	 Rickrack page 33	 Sand page 33	 Decor page 33	 Darts page 33	 Scissors page 34	 Honeycomb page 34
 Letter page 34	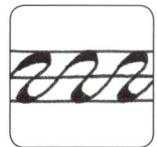 Sheet Music page 34	 Steps page 34	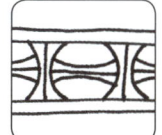 Pressure page 34	 Indian page 35	 Wind page 35	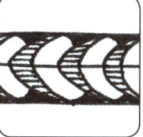 Tower page 35	 Spring page 35
 Laurel page 35	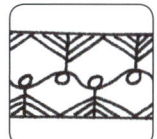 Curtain page 35	 Strips page 36	 Bird page 36	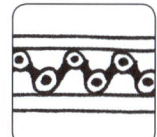 Multitude page 36	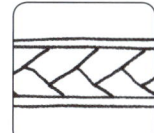 Braid page 36	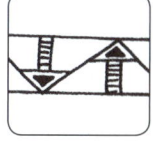 Start page 36	 Thunderstorm page 36
 Roof page 37	 Rotation page 37	 Beams page 37	 Ringlet page 37	 Cherry page 37	 Sailor's Yarn page 37		

79

SCHIFFER PUBLISHING — THE Brand for all creative Themes!

Keep creating with our full line of books and supplies from the *Painterly Days* series by author Kristy Rice

12 Colored Pencils
ISBN 978-0-7643-5167-9

18 Watercolors & Paintbrush
ISBN 978-0-7643-5168-6

Watercoloring Books for Adults
Flowers | ISBN 978-0-7643-5091-7
Patterns | ISBN 978-0-7643-5093-1
Woodlands | ISBN 978-0-7643-5092-4

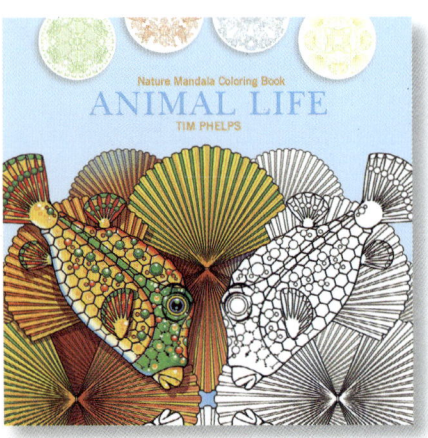

Animal Life
Nature Mandala Coloring Book,
Timothy Phelps
ISBN 978-0-7643-5278-2

Garden Life
Nature Mandala Coloring Book,
Timothy Phelps
ISBN 978-0-7643-5279-9